THE CITY OF LONDON

An outstanding photographic portrait by a gifted young photographer, this book is for those who know and love the City as well as for tourists. It is being published in association with the Corporation of London as part of the official commemoration of the 800th anniversary of the Lord Mayor of London.

One hundred striking, beautifully composed black-and-white photographs capture the famous institutions as well as the lesser-known alleys and passages of the City of London. An historical record, it also shows the extraordinary juxtaposition of old and new, characteristic of today. The richness and variety of these images, taken by the photographer of *The Magic of Kew*, will surprise and delight even the most seasoned citizen, for there is hardly ever an *expected* view of the City.

D1332966

JAMES BARTHOLOMEW

THE CITY
OF LONDON

a photographer's portrait

THE HERBERT PRESS
in association with
THE 800th ANNIVERSARY
OF THE MAYORALTY

Copyright © 1989 James Bartholomew

Copyright under the Berne Convention

First published in Great Britain 1989 by
The Herbert Press Ltd, 46 Northchurch Road, London N1 4EJ, in association
with the 800th Anniversary of the Mayoralty

Designed by Pauline Harrison
House editor: Julia MacKenzie

Printed and bound in Great Britain by Butler & Tanner Ltd, Frome, Somerset

The Map by John Flower is based on one in
the *Blue Guide to London* (A & C Black).

A CIP catalogue record for this book is available
from the British Library.

ISBN 0 906969 96 4
ISBN 0 906969 97 2 Pbk

CONTENTS

To
Jacob and Emma

ACKNOWLEDGEMENTS

I am indebted to a large number of people who have helped me with this book, and would particularly like to thank the following: Alec McGivan, Claire Bowie, Jennie Every, Jim Sewell, Chris Howell and Vivien Aldous at Guildhall; Colonel Dalton, Mark Waters and Mr Bywater, Tower Bridge; Becky Brookwell and Peter Ricketts, Mansion House; Valerie Cumming and John Schofield, Museum of London; Commander Shears, St Paul's Cathedral; Brigadier Mears and Revd John Llewellyn, Tower of London; Captain Sheehan, Inner Temple; Rear-Admiral Hill, Middle Temple; Revd Canon Robinson, Temple Church; Revd Burton Evans, St Michael, Cornhill; Revd Salter, St Dunstan in the West; Revd Preb. Chad Varah and John Salter, St Stephen Walbrook; Canon Oates and Mark Upton, St Bride; Captain Hames, Stationers' Company; John South, Merchant Taylors' Company; W. A. A. Wells, Watermen and Lightermen's Company; Mr Brayne, Ironmongers' Company; Mr Barrett, Armourers' and Braziers' Company; John Oldridge, Chapman Taylor Partners; Mr Parker, Crusader Insurance PLC; Richard Vardy, Union Discount Company of London PLC; Geoffrey Yeo, St Bartholomew's Hospital and Peter Studdert, Chief Planning Officer, Bethnal Green. The largest thank you of all must go to my wife Linda, who patiently helped me edit the prints, and helped me to keep to a tight deadline.

INTRODUCTION

Sir Christopher Collett, GBE, MA, BSc

Lord Mayor 1988–9

I am delighted to have been invited to introduce James Bartholomew's book of photographs of the City of London in the year in which we celebrate the 800th Anniversary of the Mayoralty. For those of us looking back over an 800-year span of history it is rather humbling to realise some of the buildings around us in the City, and featured in this book, have origins stretching back to AD 120 and beyond.

Over such a timescale individual lives are ephemeral, and by rarely including people in his photographs James Bartholomew reflects this. The buildings and structures he has chosen to include are largely those which have been adding to our city's history over the centuries, as opposed to the more recent additions to the landscape.

This collection represents only one person's view of the City; but via this photographer's camera we see many of the familiar sights from a different viewpoint, and are often introduced to aspects of the City of which we have been unaware or to which we do not normally have access. The fact that this is such an individual look at a fascinating city makes it all the more absorbing.

Lord Mayor

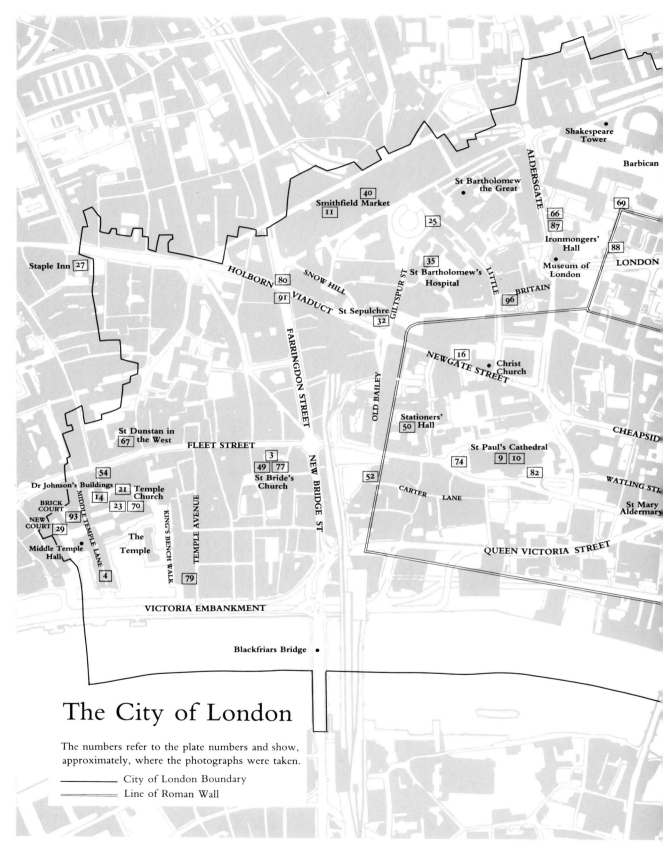

The City of London

The numbers refer to the plate numbers and show, approximately, where the photographs were taken.

———————— City of London Boundary

════════ Line of Roman Wall

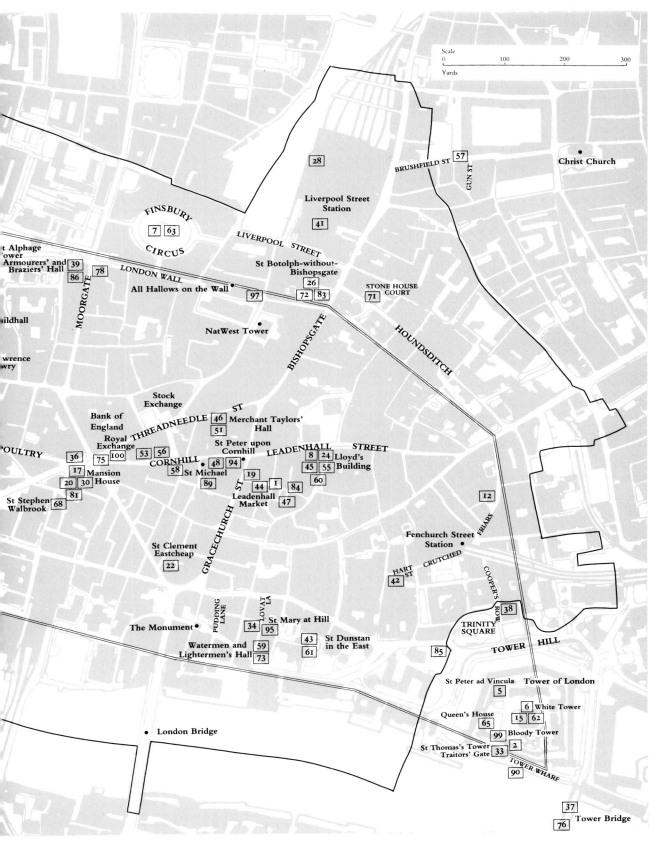

Scale
0   100   200   300
Yards

28

BRUSHFIELD ST   57   GUN ST

Christ Church

Liverpool Street
Station

FINSBURY
CIRCUS
7   63

41

LIVERPOOL STREET

t Alphage
ower
Armourers' and   39
Braziers' Hall   86   78

LONDON WALL

St Botolph-without-
Bishopsgate
26

STONE HOUSE
COURT
71

MOORGATE

All Hallows on the Wall   97

72   83

ildhall

NatWest Tower

BISHOPSGATE

HOUNDSDITCH

wrence
wry

Stock
Exchange

Bank of
England

Royal
Exchange

THREADNEEDLE   ST   46   Merchant Taylors'
Hall
51

St Peter upon
Cornhill

LEADENHALL   STREET

OULTRY   36   75   100   53   56   48   94   8   24   Lloyd's
CORNHILL   58   St Michael   45   55   Building
17   Mansion   89   60
20   30   House   19
81   44   1   84
St Stephen   68   Leadenhall   47
Walbrook   Market

GRACECHURCH   ST

12

FRIARS

Fenchurch Street
Station

St Clement
Eastcheap
22

HART   CRUTCHED
ST

42

COOPER'S   ROW

PUDDING
LANE

LOVAT
LA

St Mary at Hill
34   95

38

TRINITY
SQUARE

The Monument   43   St Dunstan
in the East

TOWER   HILL

Watermen and   59
Lightermen's Hall   73   61

85

St Peter ad Vincula   Tower of London
5

6   White Tower

London Bridge

Queen's House   15   62
65
99   Bloody Tower
St Thomas's Tower   2
Traitors' Gate   33
90   TOWER   WHARF

37   Tower Bridge
76

II

THE PLATES

PLATE NO. I: LEADENHALL MARKET ROOF

PLATE NO. 2: WELSH GUARDSMAN BADCUP, BLOODY TOWER

PLATE NO. 3: STATUE, ST BRIDE'S CHURCH

PLATE NO. 4: MIDDLE TEMPLE LANE

PLATE NO. 5: CHAPEL OF ST PETER AD VINCULA, TOWER OF LONDON

PLATE NO. 6: ROUND TURRET, WHITE TOWER

PLATE NO. 7: FINSBURY CIRCUS

PLATE NO. 8: COUNCIL TABLE, ADAM ROOM, LLOYD'S BUILDING

PLATE NO. 9: CHOIR STALLS, ST PAUL'S CATHEDRAL

PLATE NO. 10: NELSON'S TOMB, ST PAUL'S CATHEDRAL

24

PLATE NO. II: SMITHFIELD MARKET

PLATE NO. 12: STATUES, CRUTCHED FRIARS

PLATE NO. 13: ST ALPHAGE TOWER, LONDON WALL

PLATE NO. 14: DR JOHNSON'S BUILDINGS, INNER TEMPLE

PLATE NO. 15: CHAPEL OF ST JOHN, TOWER OF LONDON

PLATE NO. 16: CHRIST CHURCH GARDEN, NEWGATE STREET

PLATE NO. 17: NORTH DRAWING ROOM, MANSION HOUSE

PLATE NO. 18: ST PAUL'S CATHEDRAL FROM WATLING STREET

PLATE NO. 19: H.S. LINWOOD & SONS, LEADENHALL MARKET

PLATE NO. 20: STATUES, EGYPTIAN HALL, MANSION HOUSE

PLATE NO. 21: CHANCEL, TEMPLE CHURCH OF ST MARY

PLATE NO. 22: GRAVESTONE, ST CLEMENT EASTCHEAP

PLATE NO. 23: FACES, TEMPLE CHURCH

PLATE NO. 24: ROSTRUM, LLOYD'S BUILDING

PLATE NO. 25: GATEWAY, ST BARTHOLOMEW THE GREAT

PLATE NO. 26: STATUE, ST BOTOLPH'S CHURCH HALL, BISHOPSGATE

PLATE NO. 27: STAPLE INN

PLATE NO. 28: PLATFORM ONE, LIVERPOOL STREET STATION

PLATE NO. 29: NEW COURT, MIDDLE TEMPLE

PLATE NO. 30: GALLERY, EGYPTIAN HALL, MANSION HOUSE

44

PLATE NO. 31: MAGOG, GUILDHALL

PLATE NO. 32: DRINKING FOUNTAIN, ST SEPULCHRE

PLATE NO. 33: TRAITORS' GATE, TOWER OF LONDON

PLATE NO. 34: ST MARY AT HILL

PLATE NO. 35: THE POOR'S BOX, ST BARTHOLOMEW'S HOSPITAL

PLATE NO. 36: ESCALATOR, BANK UNDERGROUND STATION

PLATE NO. 37: TOWER BRIDGE RAISED

PLATE NO. 38: CITY WALL, COOPER'S ROW

PLATE NO. 39: STAIRCASE, ARMOURERS' AND BRAZIERS' HALL

PLATE NO. 40: MEAT HANDLER, SMITHFIELD MARKET

PLATE NO. 41: EUROPA BISTRO, LIVERPOOL STREET STATION

PLATE NO. 42: THE SHIP, HART STREET

PLATE NO. 43: THE MONUMENT FROM ST DUNSTAN IN THE EAST

PLATE NO. 44: BUBBLES, LEADENHALL MARKET

PLATE NO. 45: ADAM ROOM, LLOYD'S BUILDING

PLATE NO. 46: MERCHANT TAYLORS' HALL

PLATE NO. 47: LEADENHALL MARKET

PLATE NO. 48: DEVIL ON CORNHILL

PLATE NO. 49: ST BRIDE'S CHURCH

PLATE NO. 50: CEILING DECORATION, STATIONERS' HALL

PLATE NO. 51: GREAT PARLOUR, MERCHANT TAYLORS' HALL

PLATE NO. 52: CARTER LANE

PLATE NO. 53: GEOFFREY'S HAIRDRESSERS, CORNHILL

PLATE NO. 54: PRINCE HENRY'S ROOM, 17 FLEET STREET

PLATE NO. 55: ESCALATORS, LLOYD'S BUILDING

PLATE NO. 56: WATER PUMP, CORNHILL

PLATE NO. 57: BRUSHFIELD STREET, SPITALFIELDS

PLATE NO. 58: UNION DISCOUNT COMPANY, 39–41 CORNHILL

72

PLATE NO. 59: FIREPLACE, THE COURT ROOM,
WATERMEN AND LIGHTERMEN'S HALL

PLATE NO. 60: PEDESTRIAN ENTRANCE, LLOYD'S BUILDING

PLATE NO. 61: NORTH WALL, ST DUNSTAN IN THE EAST

PLATE NO. 62: SQUARE TURRET, WHITE TOWER

PLATE NO. 63: DRINKING FOUNTAIN, FINSBURY CIRCUS

PLATE NO. 64: ST MARY ALDERMARY

PLATE NO. 65: QUEEN'S HOUSE, TOWER OF LONDON

PLATE NO. 66: FIREPLACE, IRONMONGERS' HALL

PLATE NO. 67: QUEEN ELIZABETH STATUE, ST DUNSTAN IN THE WEST

PLATE NO. 68: ALTAR, ST STEPHEN WALBROOK

82

PLATE NO. 69: BASTION AND SHAKESPEARE TOWER, BARBICAN

ETS
REPAIRED &
BEAUTIFIED
1687

PLATE NO. 70: DETAIL OF MONUMENT IN TEMPLE CHURCH

PLATE NO. 71: STONE HOUSE COURT

PLATE NO. 72: TOMB, ST BOTOLPH BISHOPSGATE

PLATE NO. 73: MASTER'S CHAIR, WATERMEN AND LIGHTERMEN'S HALL

PLATE NO. 74: QUEEN ANNE STATUE, ST PAUL'S CATHEDRAL

PLATE NO. 75: BANK OF ENGLAND FROM BANK UNDERGROUND STATION

PLATE NO. 76: WEST WALKWAY, TOWER BRIDGE

PLATE NO. 77: VIEW FROM THE STEEPLE OF ST BRIDE

PLATE NO. 78: W. H. CULLEN, 73 MOORGATE

PLATE NO. 79: TEMPLE CHAMBERS

PLATE NO. 80: DRAGONS, HOLBORN VIADUCT

94

PLATE NO. 81: EGYPTIAN HALL, MANSION HOUSE

PLATE NO. 82: ST PAUL'S CHURCHYARD

96

PLATE NO. 83: CHURCHYARD, ST BOTOLPH BISHOPSGATE

5 THOMAS MARSH 15

PLATE NO. 84: LEADENHALL MARKET AND LLOYD'S BUILDING

PLATE NO. 85: DRAGON, TOWER HILL

PLATE NO. 86: ARMOURERS' AND BRAZIERS' HALL

PLATE NO. 87: BANQUETING HALL, IRONMONGERS' COMPANY

PLATE NO. 88: LONDON WALL

PLATE NO. 89: ST MICHAEL'S ALLEY

English Iron Cannon
This 32 pdr of Blomfield pattern was
cast in about 1800 by the Yorkshire
firm of Samuel Walker & Co. It was
intended for Sea Service or Fortress
use and is mounted on a wooden
garrison carriage dated 1864.

PLATE NO. 90: TOWER BRIDGE FROM TOWER WHARF

PLATE NO. 91: UNDER HOLBORN VIADUCT

PLATE NO. 92: POLICE BOX, GUILDHALL

PLATE NO. 93: BRICK COURT, MIDDLE TEMPLE LANE

PLATE NO. 94: SUCCUBUS, 55 CORNHILL

108

PLATE NO. 95: INTERIOR, ST MARY AT HILL

PLATE NO. 96: OLNEY AMSDEN & SONS, LITTLE BRITAIN

PLATE NO. 97: ALL HALLOWS ON THE WALL

PLATE NO. 98: EMBRACING LOVERS, GUILDHALL

PLATE NO. 99: WHITE TOWER FROM BLOODY TOWER

PLATE NO. 100: VIEW FROM THE ROYAL EXCHANGE

NOTES

PLATE NO. 1
LEADENHALL MARKET ROOF

The market dates back to the fourteenth century when poultry was ordered to be sold here. The name Leadenhall derives from the lead roof of a manor house which stood in the vicinity and was acquired by the City in 1411.

The present market was built in 1881 by Sir Horace Jones, under the 1879–80 Act for the Improvement of Leadenhall Market. The market is so well preserved that it has been used as a period film set. See also Plate Nos 19 and 47.

PLATE NO. 2
WELSH GUARDSMAN BADCUP, BLOODY TOWER

Steps lead up from Traitors' Gate to the gates of the Bloody Tower. The tower probably gained its name because it was thought the two young Princes of the Tower, Edward V and Richard, Duke of York, were murdered here in 1483.

The heavy iron portcullis on the left is one of the few left in England in working order. This is the only entrance to the inner ward of the Tower of London so the ancient Ceremony of the Keys takes place here nightly at 10 p.m. After locking the Middle Tower and Byward Tower, the Chief Yeoman Warder and escort approach the Bloody Tower. The script is always the same:

SENTRY ON GUARD: 'Halt! Who comes there?'
CHIEF YEOMAN WARDER: 'The keys.'
SENTRY: 'Whose keys?'
WARDER: 'Queen Elizabeth's keys.'
SENTRY: 'Pass Queen Elizabeth's keys, all is well.'

Guard and escort then present arms in honour of the keys. The Chief Yeoman Warder then removes his bonnet and calls 'God preserve Queen Elizabeth'. The Guard and escort all reply 'Amen'. The keys are then delivered to the resident governor.

PLATE NO. 3
STATUE, ST BRIDE'S CHURCH

This statue, one of two, comes from St Bride and Bridewell Schools and probably dates from 1711, when the school was founded. Compare his cap and book with those of the statue in Plate No. 26.

PLATE NO. 4
MIDDLE TEMPLE LANE

Middle Temple Lane divides the Middle Temple from the Inner Temple and runs between Fleet Street and Victoria Embankment. Traditionally it provided a way through the Temple to Temple Stairs on the river.

Technically the Temple is not City ground and so acts as its own rating authority. After an incident in the reign of Charles II when law students attacked a visiting Lord Mayor, the Lord Mayor asks permission to enter the Temple.

Temple Gardens Building, in the foreground, was designed by E. M. Barry (Sir Charles Barry's eldest son) in 1878–9. The buildings seen through the arch are all postwar neo-Georgian, replacing those destroyed in the war.

PLATE NO. 5
CHAPEL OF ST PETER AD VINCULA, TOWER OF LONDON

A chapel is mentioned here in 1210 but the present building dates from c. 1520. It is aptly dedicated to St Peter in chains as many former prisoners of the Tower are buried here. These include (all beheaded): Sir Thomas More (1535), Queen Anne Boleyn

(1536), Thomas Cromwell (1540), Queen Catherine Howard (1542) and Lady Jane Grey (1554).

The alabaster tomb shown was built in 1522 by Sir Richard Cholmondeley, Lieutenant of the Tower, for himself and his wife, but he died elsewhere in 1544 and no bodies were ever laid in the tomb. The tomb did serve a purpose however, because in 1876 a medieval font was found hidden inside it, possibly placed there during Cromwell's Protectorate.

PLATE NO. 6
ROUND TURRET, WHITE TOWER

This is the only round turret on top of the White Tower. It was used for five months in 1675 by Flamsteed, the first Astronomer Royal, as the Royal Observatory, until the new building at Greenwich was ready for use.

PLATE NO. 7
FINSBURY CIRCUS

The original design for the circus was suggested by George Dance the younger in 1802. The area had been a marsh (Moorfields) until the seventeenth century when the ground was raised and it became the first public park in London. The garden here is still used by the public and summer concerts are held in the bandstand. The present buildings in the Circus date from the nineteenth and early twentieth centuries. See also Plate No. 63.

PLATE NO. 8
COUNCIL TABLE, ADAM ROOM, LLOYD'S BUILDING

This magnificent room was designed by Robert Adam (1728–92) for Bowood House in Wiltshire. The room was bought by Lloyd's when the house was threatened by demolition in the fifties and installed in the 1958 building on this site.

The Adam Room was restored to its original proportions when it was incorporated in the 1986 Richard Rogers building. The Gillow table dates from about 1800 and can extend to thirty-five feet. See also Plate No. 45.

PLATE NO. 9
CHOIR STALLS, ST PAUL'S CATHEDRAL

These magnificent choir stalls are the work of Grinling Gibbons. The carving was of such perfection that John Evelyn wrote to Christopher Wren: 'there being nothing, even in nature, so tender and delicate as the flowers and festoones [sic] about it'.

The seats are used by the cathedral prebendaries, their seats marked with gold letters. The thirty prebendaries are clergymen chosen from the Diocese of London by the Bishop. The appointment used to include a piece of land but is now only an honour.

PLATE NO. 10
NELSON'S TOMB, ST PAUL'S CATHEDRAL

Admiral Lord Nelson's tomb is in the crypt of St Paul's Cathedral and is placed directly under the dome. The black marble sarcophagus was originally designed for Cardinal Wolsey but confiscated by Henry VIII and kept until used for Nelson in 1806. Head on, it looks more like a funerary urn than a sarcophagus.

PLATE NO. 11
SMITHFIELD MARKET

'Smoothfield' was used from the twelfth century as a livestock market in connection with the annual Bartholomew Fair (held c. 1123–1855) and it was a well-known execution site, particularly in Tudor times. A permanent market was established at Smithfield in 1614 and until 1855 live animals were driven in and slaughtered here. The present market was opened in 1868 and has been enlarged and modernized since then to cover ten acres. London Central Markets, as Smithfield is officially called, maintain their own police force and own the site which is leased to the Cock Tavern, open from 5.30 in the morning for the use of the market traders (or anyone else up at that hour!). See also Plate No. 40.

PLATE NO. 12
STATUE, CRUTCHED FRIARS

Crutched Friars used to have a Priory in the area and the street name derives from the red cross on the monks' habits.

The sculpture is of the same Swedish granite that was used for the building, with Italian marble for the hands, heads and feet. It was commissioned by the building's architects, Chapman Taylor Partners, and made by Michael Black in 1982 for the owners, Commercial Union Properties. Within a modern setting the monks' quiet grace renews the street's tradition.

PLATE NO. 13
ST ALPHAGE TOWER, LONDON WALL

This was the tower of the priory church of Elsing Spital, founded in 1332, which became the parish church of St Alphage after the Reformation. The church was demolished in 1923 leaving only the fourteenth-century tower. On one wall there is a memorial to Sir Rowland Hayward, twice Lord Mayor in Elizabeth I's reign.

PLATE NO. 14
DR JOHNSON'S BUILDINGS, INNER TEMPLE

These were built in 1857–8 and are so named because Dr Johnson lived in a house on this site from 1760 to 1765. On the right is the eleventh-century porch of the Temple church.

PLATE NO. 15
CHAPEL OF ST JOHN, TOWER OF LONDON

This chapel, which is in the White Tower, has been described by Pevsner as 'one of the most impressive pieces of Early Norman architecture in England'. It is a Chapel Royal and was used for royal occasions such as the lying in state of Elizabeth, Henry VII's Queen, and the betrothal of Queen Mary to Philip of Spain (Count Egmont acted as proxy).

From the reign of Charles II to 1857 the chapel was used as a storehouse for State records, but is now, again, used as a chapel.

PLATE NO. 16
CHRIST CHURCH GARDEN, NEWGATE STREET

In the thirteenth century a group of Franciscans (called Grey Friars because of the colour of their garments) came to London and established a monastery on this site. Following the dissolution of the monasteries the Grey Friars church became a parish church and was rededicated as Christ Church. The church was rebuilt by Wren after the Great Fire on the site of the chancel of the monastic church, but it was severely damaged in the Blitz. This garden is probably on the site of the nave of the earlier church.

PLATE NO. 17
NORTH DRAWING ROOM, MANSION HOUSE

In the original joiner's contract of 1749 this room is called the Common Parlour but when John Wilkes was Lord Mayor in 1774–5 it was called the Dining Parlour. It was he who gave the house five grisaille paintings, of which one, the *Toilet of Venus*, is shown here. The marble fireplace was designed by the building's architect, George Dance the elder, and executed by Christopher Horsnaile, one of the masons who worked on the Mansion House.

PLATE NO. 18
ST PAUL'S CATHEDRAL FROM WATLING STREET

Watling Street forms part of the old Roman road from Dover. It was known as Aphelingestrate in 1213 and may have become Watling Street by the mistaken addition of a 'w' by a copyist. Chaucer, in *The House of Fame*, said that the Milky Way was called 'Watlynge strete', presumably because it stretched across the sky as the road did across England.

Ye Olde Watling, on the extreme left, was established in 1666 but the present building dates from the early eighteenth century. The dome of St Paul's is well framed here, dwarfing the tower of St Augustine Watling Street. The church was destroyed in the war and the tower now forms part of St Paul's choir school.

PLATE NO. 19
H. S. LINWOOD & SONS, LEADENHALL MARKET

The market is an extraordinary enclave in the midst of the City, with fishmongers, butchers and vegetable stalls thriving, just as they have for generations. See also Plate Nos 1 and 47.

PLATE NO. 20
STATUES, EGYPTIAN HALL, MANSION HOUSE

The Mansion House was built in 1739–53, by George Dance the elder, to provide an official residence for the Lord Mayor. The Egyptian Hall is the principal room and the niches around the sides contain a remarkable collection of mid-Victorian marble statuary, depicting literary, historical and allegorial subjects. See also Plate Nos 30 and 81.

PLATE NO. 21
CHANCEL, TEMPLE CHURCH OF ST MARY

The Temple church is unusual in that it is not a parish church but a Royal Peculiar, i.e. it comes under the direct jurisdiction of the Sovereign as Head of the Church of England. The original part of the church, the Round, was built c. 1160–85. A new chancel, part of which is shown here, was built c. 1220–40 and consecrated in the presence of Henry III. It is one of the most beautiful of thirteenth-century English buildings. Benchers of the Inner Temple would sit on this south side of the choir, with ladies behind. Benchers of the Middle Temple would sit on the north side.

The monument on the right is to Richard Martin, Recorder of London, who died in 1618.

PLATE NO. 22
GRAVESTONE, ST CLEMENT EASTCHEAP

There has been a church on this site since the eleventh century but the rather plain present building dates from 1683–7 and is by Wren. It is one of the few churchyards in the middle of the City which still contains graves.

PLATE NO. 23
FACES, TEMPLE CHURCH

The left detail is part of the monument to Edmund Plowden (d. 1584), Treasurer of the Middle Temple during construction of the hall. Next to it is one of the pillars which separate the Round from the choir, with a carved head which appears to support the Purbeck marble above it. See also Plate No. 70.

PLATE NO. 24
ROSTRUM, LLOYD'S BUILDING

The Rostrum was designed by Sir Edwin Cooper for the 1928 Lloyd's building. The bell hanging within it is from HMS Lutine, a former French frigate in the service of the British Navy, which sank off the Dutch coast in 1799 on its way to Hamburg with a cargo of gold and silver. The bell was salvaged in 1859 and is rung to announce the fate of overdue vessels which have been reinsured with Lloyd's; two rings for good news, one ring for bad. It is also rung on ceremonial occasions.

PLATE NO. 25
GATEWAY, ST BARTHOLOMEW THE GREAT

The church was originally part of the priory founded in 1123, together with the hospital, by Rahere, one of Henry I's courtiers, in fulfilment of a vow made to St Bartholomew when lying sick with malaria in Rome. In a vision the Saint had appeared to save him from the clutches of a winged monster. The base of the gateway shown here was the thirteenth-century south entrance to the priory church. The nave was pulled down after the dissolution and the site made into the churchyard which can be seen through this gate. The present church, which can be seen in the distance, was formed out of the crossing, chancel and transepts of the priory church. The upper part of the gateway dates from the sixteenth century.

It is a tradition, revived in the nineteenth century, that on Good Friday twenty-one widows receive an old sixpence, placed on a flat tombstone in the churchyard.

PLATE NO. 26
STATUE, ST BOTOLPH'S CHURCH HALL, BISHOPSGATE

The statues on either side of the main door to this hall are apparently of charity school children (although they look like adults) and wear badges that show a combined date of 1825. The artificial Coade stone, of which they are made, was well known for being hard wearing and widely used for outdoor monuments until the secret of its manufacture was lost in 1840.

The hall used to be a parish infant school but its educational role ceased in 1905. In 1952 it was restored by the Worshipful Company of Fanmakers to hold their meetings in. See also Plate No. 83.

PLATE NO. 27
STAPLE INN

The origin of the name is in doubt but by 1415 the buildings had become an Inn of Chancery. In 1884 the 'Honourable Society of Staple Inn' sold the buildings and these were bought, in part, by the Prudential Assurance Co. They are let now as offices and legal chambers. The Holborn frontage retains the Tudor facade and it is an interesting example of the period.

PLATE NO. 28
PLATFORM ONE, LIVERPOOL STREET STATION

Liverpool Street Station (so called because the street outside is named after Lord Liverpool, Prime Minister 1812–27) was completed in 1875 on a site which had once been occupied by Bethlehem Hospital (Bedlam). The train shed is one of the few parts of the station which will survive the major redevelopment at present underway. See also Plate No. 41.

PLATE NO. 29
NEW COURT, MIDDLE TEMPLE

The building on the left dates from 1676. It was constructed by Dr Barbon in the former grounds of Essex House, a building which he had purchased and almost completely demolished. The association with Robert Devereux, Earl of Essex, Queen Elizabeth I's favourite, who named Essex House, continues to this day – the stuccoed building in the centre of the picture is called Devereux Chambers.

PLATE NO. 30
GALLERY, EGYPTIAN HALL, MANSION HOUSE

The stained-glass window at the east end of the Egyptian Hall was designed by Alexander Gibbs in 1868 and depicts Sir William Walworth killing Wat Tyler, and Edward VI entering the City after his coronation. See also Plate Nos 20 and 81.

PLATE NO. 31
MAGOG, GUILDHALL

The wooden statues of Gog and Magog in the Great Hall are by David Evans and replace those destroyed in the Blitz in 1940. The Gog and Magog legend is unclear, as Winston Churchill said in a 1951 speech: 'world politics, like the history of Gog and Magog, are very confused and much disputed'. One version is that there were two giants, Gogmagog and Corineus, who were combatants in a Trojan invasion of Britain, and that the former's name has been divided and the latter's forgotten. Traditionally the figures were carried in the Lord Mayor's Show.

Each Lord Mayor has his name and dates of office inscribed in the high windows of the Hall. In five years' time the City Corporation will have to find alternative space because all the windows will be full.

PLATE NO. 32
DRINKING FOUNTAIN, ST SEPULCHRE

The Metropolitan Free Drinking Fountain Association (later known as The Metropolitan Drinking Fountain and Cattle Trough Association) was founded in 1859 by Samuel Gurney, MP, nephew of the prison reformer Elizabeth Fry, to provide 'a safe and pleasant alternative to the intoxicating beverages banned by the prohibitionists'. The fountain pictured here was the first and was erected by Samuel Gurney at his own expense. It was initially on Holborn Hill but removed here when the viaduct was built in the 1860s.

St Sepulchre, between Snow Hill and Giltspur Street, first mentioned in the twelfth century, was rebuilt in the fifteenth century, and again after the Great Fire, and restored in the nineteenth century. St Sepulchre is positioned across the road from the site of Newgate prison (demolished 1902) and the bells of St Sepulchre used to ring on the day condemned prisoners were executed.

PLATE NO. 33
TRAITORS' GATE, TOWER OF LONDON

Along the south side of the Tower of London is St Thomas's Tower, named in honour of St Thomas à Becket and built in 1280. Underneath it is Traitors'

Gate, the water entrance to the Tower, through which many famous prisoners came. One prisoner who entered here but was not executed was the Princess Elizabeth, accused of treason in 1554 in connection with Wyatt's rebellion. She was ferried by boat in the rain, and fell on the stone steps protesting her innocence. There she remained for several hours until persuaded to move to more comfortable quarters.

In 1614 Lord Grey died in St Thomas's Tower after eleven years of imprisonment, and I was told by a Yeoman of the Guard that his ghost creaks the bed of the Keeper of the Crown Jewels, who lives in this tower.

PLATE NO. 34
ST MARY AT HILL

There was a church on this site in the twelfth century but the present building is by Wren (1670–6). However, the west end on Lovat Lane, shown here, was built by George Gwilt in 1787–8. Lovat Lane was originally known as Love Lane because of the prostitutes who used to frequent it. See also Plate No. 95.

PLATE NO. 35
THE POOR'S BOX, ST BARTHOLOMEW'S HOSPITAL

The site of Bart's Hospital has remained the same since its foundation by Rahere in 1123. Under its original charter the hospital was to care for poor men and women and so at some point these boxes (there is more than one) were placed about the hospital to collect money to provide for needy patients.

The lettering on the metal box has been repainted but out of line with the earlier lettering.

PLATE NO. 36
ESCALATOR, BANK UNDERGROUND STATION

The underground Waterloo & City Line, popularly known as 'the Drain', links Bank with Waterloo and provides a vital service for City workers who live in Surrey and Hampshire. Technically it is not part of the London Underground system but run by British Rail, and it has its own rolling stock.

Wooden escalators, as shown here, are being replaced on the Underground following the 1987 King's Cross fire which is believed to have started under one of the old-style escalators.

PLATE NO. 37
TOWER BRIDGE RAISED

One of the most potent tourist images of London, Tower Bridge, was designed by Sir John Wolfe Barry and Sir Horace Jones and opened in 1894 by the Prince of Wales (later Edward VII).

The hydraulic machinery that first raised the bascules was supplied by Armstrong Mitchell and went out of service in the mid 1970s. It was superseded by the present electro-oil hydraulic system which now raises the bridge using the original Victorian driveshaft and gearing. The bridge is raised about 400 times a year, and on one of these occasions, in 1952, a London double-decker bus accidentally jumped the gap.

PLATE NO. 38
CITY WALL, COOPER'S ROW

The medieval City wall, built on the Roman wall, survives here almost to its full height. The railway lines behind lead into Fenchurch Street Station.

PLATE NO. 39
STAIRCASE, ARMOURERS' AND BRAZIERS' HALL

The main staircase of Armourers' Hall dates from 1840 when the hall was rebuilt. The Company's first charter was given in 1453 by Henry VI, who was a member of the Company. The present charter, which amalgamated the Armourers and the Braziers, was granted in 1708 by Queen Anne.

Under the wooden memorial to members of the Company who died in both World Wars, is a beautiful silver working model of a knight on horseback, both in full armour. This was made in Birmingham in 1897 and was given to the Company by a benefactor.

PLATE NO. 40
MEAT HANDLER, SMITHFIELD MARKET

The listed market shed is to undergo a major refurbishment as part of the Smithfield Local Plan and will include studio flats, second-floor offices and underground parking. The Local Plan covers forty-seven acres around Smithfield and Bart's Hospital. See also Plate No. 11.

PLATE NO. 41
EUROPA BISTRO, LIVERPOOL STREET STATION

This was originally built as a tea room at the beginning of the century but its latest, and final, role was as the Europa Bistro. The plush seats under the windows provided a good place to view the station. I was sorry to hear that the Bistro had been demolished just two months after I took this picture, as part of the redevelopment of the station. See also Plate No. 28.

The Broadgate development next to the station was, at the time of construction, the largest European office development.

PLATE NO. 42
THE SHIP, HART STREET

Just along the street from St Olave's church, this small Younger's pub is easy to miss. I particularly like the grape motif over the lintel.

PLATE NO. 43
THE MONUMENT FROM ST DUNSTAN IN THE EAST

Built between 1671–7, in accordance with a 1667 Act of Parliament, to commemorate the Great Fire of 1666, the Monument is sited 202 feet from where the fire started in Pudding Lane. St Dunstan in the East, 150 yards from Pudding Lane, was rebuilt after the fire by Wren and again in the nineteenth century but was severely damaged by enemy action in 1941. The shell was made into a public garden in 1971 and laid out by the Worshipful Company of Gardeners. See also Plate No. 61.

PLATE NO. 44
BUBBLES, LEADENHALL MARKET

Bubbles is a stray cat who initially chose to belong to Linwood the fishmonger across Grand Avenue at No. 6. This upwardly mobile cat evidently prefers champagne to fish as he now lives inside H. Blankley's shop which specializes in champagne and caviar.

PLATE NO. 45
ADAM ROOM, LLOYD'S BUILDING

This room is used by the Lloyd's Council and Committee. I only had one chance to visit and decided to use two pictures which accentuated the furniture and curtains, from a total of four. See also Plate No. 8.

PLATE NO. 46
MERCHANT TAYLORS' HALL

The present Merchant Taylors' Hall dates from the 1950s and was designed by Sir Albert Richardson after the previous building had been bombed in September 1940, but the stonework and foundations of the 1347 Hall still exist beneath the new building. The bronze chandeliers were also to Sir Albert's design and replace those of Waterford crystal destroyed in the Blitz.

The organ was made in London in 1722 and after various homes ended up in Dartford from where it was brought by the Company. It was rebuilt by Noel Manders, a new case made, and installed in 1966. See also Plate No. 51.

PLATE NO. 47
LEADENHALL MARKET

Leadenhall market occupies part of the site of the Roman basilica and forum built late in the first century AD. The basilica, which was a town hall and law court, was about the length of St Paul's Cathedral and straddled the present Gracechurch Street. The forum was the civic centre and main market place and it is interesting to note that 2000 years later a market exists on the same site. See also Plate Nos 1 and 19.

PLATE NO. 48
DEVIL ON CORNHILL

I had to go up to the roof of St Peter upon Cornhill to get the best shot of this strange beast. I had seen him from the north side of Cornhill, perched on top of No. 55 and leering down at the street. The wire around his middle is to stop him from falling, but it almost seems like a harness to prevent the 'devil' from leaping down and attacking passers-by. See also Plate No. 94.

PLATE NO. 49
ST BRIDE'S CHURCH

The church is the only one in London dedicated to the sixth-century Irish saint, St Bridget, whose name has here been anglicized. The present building, the eighth on the site, was designed by Sir Christopher Wren and although badly damaged in 1940, has been restored.

The church has been called the 'printers' cathedral' and is the journalists' church. The association with those 'in the print' stems from the arrival c.1500 of Wynken de Worde, who set up a press in the churchyard because many people of importance (i.e. those who could read) lived in this area. See also Plate No. 77.

PLATE NO. 50
CEILING DECORATION, STATIONERS' HALL

The Stationers' Company was established in 1403 and incorporated by Royal Charter in 1557. It is one of the few Companies whose members have some connection with their so-called trade. Even Prince Charles, who is a liveryman of this Company, has had his work published. Until the Copyright Act of 1911 was passed, the compulsory registration of all books for copyright took place at Stationers' Hall.

The present Hall is on the site of Abergavenny House, purchased by the Company in 1611. The post-fire building was severely damaged in World War II and subsequently restored; this included reconstructing this ceiling to its 1800 design.

PLATE NO. 51
GREAT PARLOUR, MERCHANT TAYLORS' HALL

Granted a Royal Charter in 1327 the Company traditionally consisted of tailors and linen armourers. It had the authority to check its own members as there was much swindling of lengths sold at market. The Company still has a silver yard of 1503. The Company has had no real connection with its trade since the seventeenth century and members have been more general merchants. Like other livery companies it supports charitable causes including education; Merchant Taylors' School is wholly owned by the Company, for example.

The Great Parlour is an exact copy of the one in the 1682 Hall destroyed in the Blitz. See also Plate No. 46.

PLATE NO. 52
CARTER LANE

A wall enclosing the precinct of the medieval St Paul's Cathedral once stood on the site of Carter Lane.

The reflection in the window on the left is of the steeple of St Bride. See also Plate No. 77.

PLATE NO. 53
GEOFFREY'S HAIRDRESSERS, CORNHILL

This men's hairdressers has remained virtually unchanged since it opened in 1934. Lionel Lee, the present proprietor, has worked here since then and has been barber to forty Lord Mayors during his long career.

PLATE NO. 54
PRINCE HENRY'S ROOM, 17 FLEET STREET

The building dates from 1610, when it was constructed as part of a tavern. The Jacobean plaster ceiling shown here is one of the finest in London and was one of the few to survive the Great Fire. At its centre can be seen the Prince of Wales's feathers and the initials 'PH' enclosed within a star-shaped border. This may give a clue as to why the room is so-called; a few months before the house was built Prince Henry, James I's elder son, was created Prince of Wales, the first for a hundred years.

When the London County Council became interested in acquiring the building at the end of the last century, this room was being used as a barber's shop. Restoration revealed the half-timbered front and apart from the ground floor, which had to be set back from the road, the building looks much as it did in 1610.

PLATE NO. 55
ESCALATORS, LLOYD'S BUILDING

This is taken inside the controversial new Lloyd's building, designed by Richard Rogers. This is the third building on the site, all built this century.

Between 1796 and 1928 (when its first building, by Sir Edwin Cooper, was complete) Lloyd's Corporation occupied premises in the Royal Exchange.

PLATE NO. 56
WATER PUMP, CORNHILL

This pump dates from 1799 and is on the site of a well of 1282. The pump was erected after contributions were gathered from the Bank of England, the East India Company, neighbouring fire offices, bankers and traders of the ward of Cornhill.

PLATE NO. 57
BRUSHFIELD STREET, SPITALFIELDS

Christ Church, at the end of Brushfield Street, was paid for by a tax on coal, designed by Nicholas Hawksmoor and completed in 1729. The area was a centre of Huguenot immigration and they established a silk-weaving industry here. Many of the houses they inhabited are now listed buildings.

Prior to 1641 the Honourable Artillery Company shared a training ground in this area with the Gunners of the Tower, a fact reflected in the street names – Artillery Lane and Gun Street (the latter can be seen in the photograph).

PLATE NO. 58
UNION DISCOUNT COMPANY, 39–41 CORNHILL

The Union Discount Company of London PLC was formed in 1885 when the General Credit and Discount Company of London Ltd merged with the United Discount Corporation; the knot on the crest hanging outside the building symbolizes the merger. The five bezants represent banking, the company being one of the eight houses that comprise the London discount market. After the union of the two companies the present site was acquired and this building by John MacVicar Anderson was opened in 1890.

This view looks west along the south side of Cornhill with the Mappin & Webb building in the distance on the extreme right.

PLATE NO. 59
FIREPLACE, THE COURT ROOM, WATERMEN AND LIGHTERMEN'S HALL

Designed by William Blackburn and completed in 1780, this building was one of the guild halls to survive the Blitz.

The mantelpiece is of marble with a carving of the god Thames. Above is the coat of arms granted by Elizabeth I in 1585 which bears the motto (translated): At Commandment of Our Superiors. The patterned carpet, interestingly, was made to order in 1961 by six Persian girls living in exile in Bulgaria.

PLATE NO. 60
PEDESTRIAN ENTRANCE, LLOYD'S BUILDING

This is an access ramp that forms part of the Lime Street entrance to the new Lloyd's building. This ramp was the site of Benbridge's Inn.

PLATE NO. 61
NORTH WALL, ST DUNSTAN IN THE EAST

St Dunstan's tower and the shell of the nave were restored in 1971. The overall plans included a garden with many benches and a fountain, and the atmosphere is quiet and subdued, as if the people who come here do so for the opportunity of church-like contemplation. See also Plate No. 43.

PLATE NO. 62
SQUARE TURRET, WHITE TOWER

This view from the top of the White Tower in the Tower of London looks northwest towards the City. In the foreground on Trinity Square is Sir Edwin Cooper's impressive 1922 building for the Port of London Authority. Behind it, to the left, are the new Lloyd's building and the NatWest Tower.

PLATE NO. 63
DRINKING FOUNTAIN, FINSBURY CIRCUS

Erected in 1902 by the Metropolitan Drinking Fountain and Cattle Trough Association, the stone fountain with four spigots is housed in a wooden shelter with a tiled roof. In the background on the left is the bandstand where summer concerts are held. See also Plate Nos 7 and 32.

PLATE NO. 64
ST MARY ALDERMARY

John Stow, writing at the end of the sixteenth century, says the church was so called because it was 'elder than any church of St Marie in the City'. The church was rebuilt by Wren after the Fire.

On the left can be seen part of St Mary le Bow, one of Wren's finest steeples. Those born within sound of the Bow Bells are said to be true Cockneys.

PLATE NO. 65
QUEEN'S HOUSE, TOWER OF LONDON

This charming group of half-timbered buildings was built in the reign of Henry VIII. Queen Anne Boleyn is said to have spent her last night here before being executed and Guy Fawkes and his accomplices were examined in the council chamber in 1605.

The Queen's House was also the scene of one of the most daring escapes from the Tower. Lord Nithsdale, on the eve of his execution in 1716, was visited by his wife who masterminded his escape dressed as one of her lady's maids.

PLATE NO. 66
FIREPLACE, IRONMONGERS' HALL

The present Hall was opened in 1925, replacing the one destroyed by a German daylight bombing raid in 1917. The Hall is in Tudor style, giving an overall impression of a sixteenth-century house. On the left is the dowry chest of Ann Kent, wife of Izaak Walton, author of *The Compleat Angler* and a member of the Company. See also Plate No. 87.

PLATE NO. 67
QUEEN ELIZABETH STATUE, ST DUNSTAN IN THE WEST

A church was first mentioned on this site in 1237 but the present octagonal building dates from 1829–33. The statue of Elizabeth dates from 1586 and was originally on the Ludgate, halfway up Ludgate Hill. When this was pulled down in 1760 the statue was moved to St Dunstan in the West.

PLATE NO. 68
ALTAR, ST STEPHEN WALBROOK

Wren's church of 1672–9 is on the east side of Walbrook but there had been a church on the west side as early as 1096. The church is one of Wren's masterpieces and in at least one respect was a trial run for St Paul's. Henry Moore's travertine marble altar was put in place as part of the nine-year restoration of the church, completed in 1987.

In 1953 the present vicar, the Revd Preb. Chad Varah, started the Samaritans in the vestry of the church and from 1964–87 they operated from the crypt.

PLATE NO. 69
BASTION AND SHAKESPEARE TOWER, BARBICAN

A Roman fort was built in this area c. AD 120, some sixty years before the city wall into which it was incorporated. The bastions of the wall which now remain mostly date from the late Middle Ages.

The Shakespeare Tower is one of three blocks of flats which form part of the Barbican complex of housing and public buildings. At the time of construction these towers were the highest blocks of flats in Europe.

PLATE NO. 70
DETAIL OF MONUMENT IN TEMPLE CHURCH

This is a detail of the monument, sited between the chancel and nave, to Edmund Plowden (d. 1584), the Treasurer of the Middle Temple. I particularly like the image of the young boy sitting on a skull. See also Plate No. 23.

PLATE NO. 71
STONE HOUSE COURT

Stone House Court is at the Bishopsgate end of Houndsditch. Stone House, built in 1927, is described by Pevsner as 'interesting as beginning to take notice of the approaching modern style'.

PLATE NO. 72
TOMB, ST BOTOLPH BISHOPSGATE

This is the tomb of Sir William Rawlins (1752–1838), an upholsterer who was Sheriff of London and

Middlesex in 1801–2. His 'exertion mainly contributed to the erection of a spacious building for the children of the ward schools'. The successor to that building can be seen in Plate Nos 26 and 83. The tower of the church can be seen reflected in the office building behind the tomb.

PLATE NO. 73
MASTER'S CHAIR, WATERMEN AND LIGHTERMEN'S HALL

This Sheraton-style chair was given by the Rulers of the Company in 1800 and has been used by the Masters ever since. The Royal coat of arms at the top was carved from one piece of wood.

PLATE NO. 74
QUEEN ANNE STATUE, ST PAUL'S CATHEDRAL

The present cathedral, the third on the site, was started in 1675 and declared complete in 1711 by Parliament. The west towers were amongst the last parts to be finished and apparently there were to have been two clocks, but the space for one remains to this day.

The statue of Queen Anne is a 1886 copy of Francis Bird's 1709–11 monument. The statues below represent England, Ireland, France and America.

PLATE NO. 75
BANK OF ENGLAND FROM BANK UNDERGROUND STATION

Founded by Royal Charter in 1694, the Bank, which to this day is the Government's banker, acquired its present site in 1724. Sir John Soane's one-storey building of 1788–1808 was substantially rebuilt by Sir Herbert Baker in 1921–37 making it a seven-storey building leaving only Soane's screen-walls. The portico on Threadneedle Street pictured here was Baker's work with a representation of Britannia, by Charles Wheeler, on the pediment.

PLATE NO. 76
WEST WALKWAY, TOWER BRIDGE

The high walkways between the north and south towers of the bridge were a public right of way granted by Act of Parliament when the bridge opened in 1894. However, because the bascules opened and shut faster than originally anticipated, pedestrians were able to use the bridge, and the walkways fell into disuse. They were closed before World War I.

The walkways were enclosed in glass and reopened in 1982, and provide marvellous views up and down the river.

PLATE NO. 77
VIEW FROM THE STEEPLE OF ST BRIDE

The steeple dates from 1701 and is Wren's highest despite losing eight feet when struck by lightning in 1764. It is reputed to be the inspiration for the original tiered wedding cake, made by William Rich (1755–1811), who lived at 3, Ludgate Hill.

This is the view looking east over Ludgate Hill to St Paul's. Despite new building in recent years, the dome of St Paul's still dominates the landscape. See also Plate Nos 49 and 52.

PLATE NO. 78
W. H. CULLEN, 73 MOORGATE

Moorgate was not one of the original city gates and a small postern was only made into a gate in 1415, here at the junction with London Wall. The name derives from the moor (Moorfields) onto which it gave and which was used by the local inhabitants as a rubbish tip. The gate was demolished in 1761.

PLATE NO. 79
TEMPLE CHAMBERS

This building is in Temple Avenue, backing on to King's Bench Walk, Inner Temple. Despite the name it is not part of the Temple but, inevitably, does house some solicitors' offices. The British Journal of Photography also has its offices here.

PLATE NO. 80
DRAGONS, HOLBORN VIADUCT

Dragons feature in the City of London coat of arms because in legend a dragon lived in the Thames and acted as guardian of the City. The viaduct also has four bronze statues representing Commerce, Agriculture, Science and Fine Art.

PLATE NO. 81
EGYPTIAN HALL, MANSION HOUSE

The Egyptian Hall was modelled after the so-called Egyptian Hall of Vitruvius which, in fact, bore no resemblance to Egyptian architecture. An Egyptian Hall is characterized by giant columns and a clerestory above. This room was altered by the younger Dance in 1795, introducing the tunnel-vault in place of the clerestory and flat ceiling.

PLATE NO. 82
ST PAUL'S CHURCHYARD

This stone building is in the south churchyard of St Paul's and is an entrance to the crypt of St Gregory by St Paul's. This was a church which stood south of the west front of the medieval cathedral but was not rebuilt after the Great Fire.

PLATE NO. 83
CHURCHYARD, ST BOTOLPH BISHOPSGATE

This picture shows the statue of the charity girl which is the pair to the boy in Plate No. 26.

The church was rebuilt by James Gould and George Dance the elder in 1727–9. See also Plate No. 72.

PLATE NO. 84
LEADENHALL MARKET AND LLOYD'S BUILDING

The view at this end of Grand Avenue provides a wonderful juxtaposition of Horace Jones's 1881 market and Richard Rogers's 1986 Lloyd's building.

PLATE NO. 85
DRAGON, TOWER HILL

These markers are to be found at the city boundaries. Not as grand as the city gates demolished in the eighteenth century, they serve, nonetheless, to remind us that we are entering the oldest part of London and one with very particular privileges and traditions. See also Plate No. 80.

PLATE NO. 86
ARMOURERS' AND BRAZIERS' HALL

The Hall was built in 1840 but the interior was extensively altered and decorated in 1872. The Company has a representative collection of armour and a large and important collection of plate. See also Plate No. 39.

PLATE NO. 87
BANQUETING HALL, IRONMONGERS' COMPANY

The Ironmongers' Company is one of the twelve Great Livery Companies of the City of London and dates from the fourteenth century. The heraldic crests of members who have become Lord Mayor are recorded on the windows, the most recent being Sir Greville Spratt, Lord Mayor 1987–8. Every year the arms of the new Master of the Company are carved out of the oak panelling around the hall. See also Plate No. 66.

PLATE NO. 88
LONDON WALL

The section of nineteenth-century wall on the right follows the line of the west wall of the Roman fort on this site (see Plate No. 69). St Paul's Cathedral can be seen in the distance.

PLATE NO. 89
ST MICHAEL'S ALLEY

The first London Coffee House opened in St Michael's Alley in 1652, starting a fashion among men of learning, politicians and merchants. Coffee Houses grew in number and influence and, surviving Charles II's attempt to suppress them in 1675, became an integral part of the social and trading life of the times. The Jamaica Coffee House in St Michael's Alley was used as a base for exchanging news by traders with interests in the West Indies, and today the association with the West Indies continues, at least in name, with the Jamaica Wine House.

The tower of St Michael Cornhill can be seen at the top of the picture.

PLATE NO. 90
TOWER BRIDGE FROM TOWER WHARF

This view can hardly have changed in nearly a hundred years. Salutes are fired from here on state occasions by the Honourable Artillery Company of the City of London. This is the oldest military body in the country, incorporated in 1537. See also Plate Nos 37 and 76.

PLATE NO. 91
UNDER HOLBORN VIADUCT

William Haywood's iron bridge was built to span the valley between Holborn and Newgate Street and was opened by Queen Victoria in 1869. It was one of the greatest of Victorian street improvements, overcoming the steep descent into the Holborn valley.

This view is in Farringdon Street, looking north, and shows some of the massive cast-iron work of the viaduct. The wine shop on the right extends deep into the cellars. See also Plate No. 80.

PLATE NO. 92
POLICE BOX, GUILDHALL

This blue police box is at the entrance to Guildhall Yard and against the wall of St Lawrence Jewry, the official church of the City Corporation.

Guildhall, Hall of the Corporation of the City of London, dates from c. 1411–40 but the front, shown here, is by George Dance the younger and dates from 1788–9. The modern entrance to the left is by Sir Giles Gilbert Scott and dates from the 1970s.

PLATE NO. 93
BRICK COURT, MIDDLE TEMPLE LANE

Brick Court lies to the west of Middle Temple Lane, and it is said to have been the first brick building in the Temple, hence its name. The present buildings date from the nineteenth and twentieth centuries.

This view is looking south down Middle Temple Lane. The symbol above the doorway is the Agnus Dei (Lamb of God) and flag used by the Knights Templars, who moved to this site c. 1160, and adopted by the Middle Temple as its badge.

PLATE NO. 94
SUCCUBUS, 55 CORNHILL

This creature sits on a Victorian building dating from 1893. It does not have pointed ears or a beard like the 'devil' (Plate No. 48) which appears on the same building; the breasts identify it as a succubus, a mythical female demon who sexually attacks sleeping men.

This kind of sculpture was very popular with church builders before the Great Fire and with the Victorians.

PLATE NO. 95
INTERIOR, ST MARY AT HILL

Wren rebuilt this medieval church in 1670–6 after the Great Fire had destroyed all but the tower and some walls. Another fire in the 1840s damaged the interior which was delicately restored with splendid woodwork. It was one of the most gorgeous and least spoiled interiors of all the City churches until a third fire early in 1988 ruined much of the panelling and cost the church its entire roof. I was able to photograph the interior in July 1988 while builders were beginning repairs.

PLATE NO. 96
OLNEY AMSDEN & SONS, LITTLE BRITAIN

Little Britain was a centre for booksellers from 1575 to 1725 when Paternoster Row took over this role. The street was the setting for the office of Jaggers, the lawyer in Charles Dickens's *Great Expectations*, and there are some good descriptions of the locality in the novel.

The part of Little Britain between Aldersgate Street and King Edward Street is being redeveloped. The north side of the street includes some listed buildings and these fronts will be preserved; unfortunately this is not the case for the Olney Amsden & Sons building, which will be destroyed.

PLATE NO. 97
ALL HALLOWS ON THE WALL

All Hallows on the Wall, on the left, is so called because it flanks London Wall, and in fact the vestry stands on a bastion of the Roman wall, hence its circular shape. The church was built in 1765–7 by George Dance the younger, when he was just twenty-four years old.

PLATE NO. 98
EMBRACING LOVERS, GUILDHALL

The sculpture, *Embracing Lovers*, by David Wynne, stands in the main entrance to Guildhall. Behind it is a bust of Prince Charles, wearing the crown of his investiture as Prince of Wales, also by David Wynne. This new entrance to Guildhall was designed by Sir Giles Gilbert Scott and completed in 1974.

PLATE NO. 99
WHITE TOWER FROM BLOODY TOWER

The White Tower was built c. 1078–97 although the windows were remodelled in the eighteenth century. The building is of Caen stone and was originally whitewashed, hence the tower's name. The medieval stone wall on the right formed part of the inner bailey wall.

PLATE NO. 100
VIEW FROM THE ROYAL EXCHANGE

The existing Royal Exchange building was designed by William Tite and opened by Queen Victoria in 1844 and, like its two predecessors, was used by London merchants in commerce and finance. It is not known exactly when the last bargain was struck, but business at the Exchange gradually died out at the turn of this century. The building is now mainly occupied by the Guardian Royal Exchange Assurance, although the London International Futures Exchange also has offices here and so, fittingly, the building still partly carries out the function for which it was originally built.

The three buildings seen in the photograph are, left to right: the Mansion House, Mappin & Webb, built in 1870, and Sir Edwin Cooper's interwar National Westminster Bank building. The war memorial in the foreground dates from 1919 and is by Aston Webb with sculpture by Alfred Drury. As this is one of the main intersections in the City, the steps of the Royal Exchange are one of the places from which a new sovereign is proclaimed.